for
W...

Birds' Nests
&
Other Poems

Michael McCarthy

Michael Mc Carthy

bradshaw books
Cork

Acknowledgements

Literary journals where poems have appeared include:
Céide, Poetry Ireland Review, The SHOp, Cork Literary Review, Other Poetry, Oxford Magazine, Poetry Life, The Reader, The Tablet, Other Voices, Queens Quarterly, Quest, Stroll of Poets Anthology, The Fiddlehead.

Work has also been broadcast on *The Alberta Anthology*, and BBC Radio.

Childrens' Books in Verse: *The Story of Noah and the Ark* and *The Story of Daniel in the Lions Den* published by Barefoot Books have been translated into fifteen languages.

A Travel Bursary was awarded in 1996 by Northern Arts, Newcastle on Tyne.

My thanks go to Máire Bradshaw and Liz Willows at Bradshaw Books, and to Wendy Dison for her kindness in allowing use of her image "Ash" for the cover.

Birds' Nests
&
Other Poems

First published in 2003

bradshaw books
Tigh Filí Arts Centre
Thompson House
MacCurtain Street
Cork, Ireland
Phone +353 21 4509274
Fax +353 21 4551617
e-mail bradshawbooks@cwpc.ie
Web www.tighfili.com

British Library Cataloguing in Publication Data
ISBN 0 949010 86 3

Cover art 'Ash' Wendy Dison, by kind permission of the artist
Tel: 027 66363 E: milvientos@eircom.net
Cover design, typeset and layout by Liz Willows
Printed and bound by Betaprint, Dublin

Contents

I
Birds' Nests

II
Not Written on Stone

The Gift

The small miracles that transform life are offered almost by accident.
I give thanks for those whose happening upon me made poetry possible.

In memory of my mother

I

Birds' Nests

METANOIA

Let me be mad for awhile
unhinged; by some passion
made daring and deliberate

lured into the heart's motion
into the wild asunder
the broad and daredevil sky

inebriate with longing
mad with love or poetry
the dangerous delirium of flying.

In this madness we will meet
young in our reckless hopes
old in our dreaming

shaken loose and shocked
we'll sorrow, salt our crying.
We will not regret

how it made us different
changed our looking hearts
until we could see blind.

INHERITANCE

Strong the hard road
of the man who walks
to the hollow of his thirst
where as a child he rode trees
bareback, plunged his appetites
in the wet fern behind the well
and in the privacy of ditches
learned the languages of skin
from the rough bark of trees
from the pigs
back-side to the wind
nose to the ground
rooting the sod
turning the clod
the clay earthy and ringing.

That freshness was frocked over
by the crust of time, the clerical collar.
The smells were lost:
bank of turf, sour milk, horse sweat
embrocation in the bedroom
the new skin of *bonhams*
after their birthing in the night
and in the morning at their frantic
scamper for suck until
standing in rows neat as eggs
the sow warped the milk
into their sinews.

Going below ground now
he claims his inheritance
where the earth is black
and the black is rich
and the rich is flesh
blood and bone
socket and hock
tough as tank
and soft as
the salamandering morning.

RERAHANAGH

Awake again, and full of fire
in the belly, in the blood.
Under the fingernails
of the bridge the greening creeps

between the cracks of mortar
in the underside of those echo chambers
between the river and the sky.
I long for the fuschias

red and bleeding honey
for the scrawny yellow-legged hens
and stony ditches scratched loose
beside the gable

for the rough-hewn stone
flat-flagged upward to the barn
where the hedge turned the corner
and bikes bumped on the rising road.

I move into the narrowing boreen
between the briars that
tentacle towards each other
where the *bad woman* was sent in flight

along with her imaginary terror
and the hell-to-pay moment
of mother-rage comforted
this frightened child.

Here, in the night
I long for feathers
for the nest with small bird's eggs
in the barely audible ditches.

THE VISIT
for Kathleen

He came down the road
riding his iron-wheeled spider.
It clanked and squeaked
through the gap
into the potato field by the river.
He filled its belly with the blue spill.
The heavy-hoofed horse
reins guided by his big farmery hands
hauled it through the drills.
The spray came hissing
through its dozen nozzles
settled on the stalks' white flower.
The angel of blight would pass over
leaving this crop unharmed.
At evening two wooden barrels stood
fat-bellied by the riverbank
emptied except for the shovel handle,
the strong smell of bluestone, sulphate.

Time for bed, my sister said
as she swept the kitchen
to a spick and span.
It wasn't time for bed at all.
Upstairs, we lie by the window
sulking. With our nails
we carelessly carve careful shapes
on last year's hardened candle-spill.
We hear a rattle down the stony road,
wheels hissing on the gravel.
The spraying machine man
leans his bike against the hedge.
There is whispering.
His white raincoat shines.
A great ball of moon rises
over Jackie Kingston's hill.

SAM GOSLING'S CORNER

Sam Gosling's orchard was hidden
in the growth behind the grain loft.
The trick would be to wake Sam first,
not have him woken by a squall of cats.
Our bare feet made no sound
on the cold flagged floor,

there was only the ticking of the clock
and Sam's afternoon snore.
"What's the time Sir?"
(The Master said his name was Mister Gosnell
and we should call him Sir.)
"What's the time Sir?" "Half past three", he said.

The apple trees were friendly,
familiar like his trousers of grey frieze.
We took an apple each and ran
back past his house, and heard him
talking to himself: "Isn't that the devil now
the kettle boiled, the tay ready, and no bread."

We ate them all the way to Kingston's bridge,
compared our teeth marks on the cores;
then raced them down the river at the count of three.
Mine was winning till it sank.
You could tell an apple from its taste
we said. Sam's tasted, sort of, Protestant.

Shop apples seduced us after that.
They were from foreign parts
had painted lips and polished skin.
Their taste had no religion.

BIRDS' NESTS

We learned about God
from birds' nests; from those
tabernacles perched in a hedge,
hidden between moss covered stones
in a ditch, or under the lip of some ledge.

When you found one, it was a secret
you kept to yourself. I had seven that were mine.
My brother had more but he was bigger than me
and anyway crows didn't count. They were too high up.
You had to be able to see into them. My uncle lifted me up
to see into one that had blue eggs in it. That counted alright.
My mother said the one I showed her was a robin's nest.
Her breast was red because she had felt sorry for Our Lord
on the cross, and blood dripped from the nail onto her breast
and the spot never came off.

You had to whisper. It was like being in Church.
Touching the eggs was a sin.
It was like lifting a girl's skirt.
I put my hand in once
just to see how they felt. They were
smooth like my sister's hair
warm like her skin.
I told it in confession, said I'd never do it again.

Donegan lived near the school.
He said birds' nests were a cod.
He robbed the one in the wall,
stuck his hand right into the hole
it came out with the eggs in his fist.
We could hear the cracking of shells
see the ooze through his fingers like sick.
His face had a crooked look.

He wiped the egg off his hand on Mary Driscoll's dress.

DUMB

The fat white meat of the salted pig
stares back at me from the plate. Eat that.
I shuffle turnips with my fork.
Eat it, he says.

Gripping my eyes I swallow, trying
to not feel the hairy stubble on my tongue.
Call your sister a liar would you. Slap.
My cheek burns with the sting.

The bull roars from his belly,
gores the ditch.
I smell a dank stick
crack it with my fist.

The fat frog in the hayfield
squats; staring; dumb.
Beside him, in the stubble
his amputated arms and legs.

STREET SCENE

His brown cardboard face has bristles
ten days old.
He smells of stale porter; piss.
The fork of his trousers sags.
His knees are slightly bent
for balance.

His bed last night was
a wheelbarrow in Nagle's yard.
Now he's a gathering of stiffnesses
as he shambles past Fallons' shop
with its fol-de-dols and fishing rods.

The buns in Miss O Mahony's window
are keeping their heads down.
The street is a stretch of rope.
The houses are made of rubber.

At the Square, he apologises to himself
slurs through his pockets
for something
his memory can't quite pick out.

You could hear the thud from Sheehy's Bar.
"There was no need for that.
What was that for?"
The telegraph pole doesn't say a word.

ACROSS THE RIVER
i.m. Peggy Kingston

From the bank at our side I see green *gramalia*.
Long strands stretch downstream under curves of glass.
At the river-bend the ash tree shudders
the air is thickened by a family of mallards
flying out suddenly, following their arrows.

Upstream a heron stands on stilts
looks across, sees Willie Kingston's ghost
sinewy as ever
and walking with his sinewy stick
following cows from one field to another.

I saw you, his son, last spring.
You were walking with a stick
and she was with you.
You went at convalescent pace.
You've reached the age your father was.

Soon I too will be old
but for now I am a boy again.
We're on our way from school
and you are in the slate-roofed shed
tending to your tractor.

You're rubbing rust spots with waste oil
preserving it. The blackened oil creeps
inside the cracks across your knuckles.
Tonight you'll have to scrub your hands
and nails if you're going dancing.

We've heard the news at school.
She comes from west along, and
she's a teacher. Her name is
Peggy Hayes we say, and watch
your eyes, your face become a circle.

And now I hear a different news.
I see the circle broken.
We'll watch for her
where ghosts drive cows
across from *Poll-Na-Guella*.

VISITATION

We were standing inside the stall doorway.
We had finished milking.
There was a sense of someone missing.
Through the opening, with the sun behind him
a young man in farmer's clothes:
the gansey with the sleeves unravelled
the shirt without the collar,
was standing on the dung heap.

He said a dove would come.
And then a pigeon.
And after that an eagle.
And then, a dove again.

In no time, there she was
the colour of white dust
perched on the row of evergreens
in the field below the house.
Like milk music, it couldn't
have been coincidence.
When the pigeon came, I knew
we were as good as numbered.

He flew in at a kind of slant
turned north towards the haggard,
and by the time he landed
on the elbow of the elm tree
he had turned into an eagle.
The feathers of his underwing
had changed into a rowan-berry red.
They glowed like flowers.

Below him by the straw rick
there were moss grown jars and crockery.
Before the second dove appeared
Your coming was as certain as translucency.

HOSANNA

I

Seventeen seals came in to Tragumna the Sunday before Christmas.
We were the boys on the rocks. We were shepherds.
We were anything we wanted to be.
Our eyes were the moon looking over Carbery.
There was light coming out of us.
Those were dark days, cloaked in sycamores.
These were silver times between the seal shoal and the shore.
Caesar Augustus was taking a census.
We were counting miracles.
One surfaced by the corner of the island.
She was big as Bethlehem.
Another nearer the rocks was dappled.
The rest rolled where the white crests of the waves
were woolly, and the sea swaddled them.

II

Joseph set out for a hard town, its streets foreign as frost.
Mary had a rounded face, had the strength of a sapling.
She was carrying her child.
She was giving birth
as he stood close, helpless in his big shoes
and watched the tightening of her fingers.
His careful calloused hands knew the rhythms of timber.
The urgencies of labour and birth were a different river.
And the doors were closed, and the clouds were shifting.
Shepherds were watching their flocks.
And suddenly
a great throng of seals were singing:
Glory to God in the highest heavens
and in the sea's deepest.

THE ANGEL

I'm in my nurse's navy blue;
I see the old man's chest is bad.
His emphysema's acting up.
He sucks at insubstantial air
takes nervous sips
then blows out tiny puffs
his lips the shape it takes to whistle.
I tease about his cigarettes
then wheel him out.

The surgeon in green smock, white mask
across his mouth, prepares himself.
On the table this man, middle aged.
I see silver on his shaven chin
a star on his forehead, tiny relic
of some childhood knock.

I take his soft strong hand, tell him
he'll soon sleep; he'll not remember anything.
His eyes return my look and draw me in.
We swim awhile, inside each others
deep blue pools.
I watch him drifting into sleep.

Soon, I'll wake up. Remember:
how he spoke my name
called me highly favoured.
How I answered yes.

THE CAVE

Nomads welcome me to their patch of valley;
give me camel's milk and shelter.
I breakfast on dates, then
walk all day till tiredness comes.

I don't sleep well.
The man who'd passed lewd looks
comes back in my dreams.
His eyes are empty.
There is hunger
along the line of his chin.
His lips move soundlessly
like goats whispering.

When I awake
it is not Jericho but a cave.
Shadows cling to the clefts in the roof
sharp edges catch the gathering of light.

A sleeping raven stirs, stretches
his black wings showing streaks of white.
Momentarily our eyes meet.

ELIZABETH

She sits under the olives in front of the house
where the land dips in terraces of rock.
Her face is full, her skin
blotched and high with colour.
Her speckled smock hangs loosely
over sandals made of camel skin.

She hears his shuffle as he moves
panniers of almonds, dried figs.
She smells his memory
the whiff of incense mixed with sweat.

She weaves papyrus into a Moses basket
with her sinewy insistent fingers.
When it is finished he will line it
with bitumen and pitch.
In the fading light, purple gathers
round her eyes.
His silence puzzles her.

HER GALILEE STONE

As the evening is drained of light
and dusk thickens, she hears:
in the sharp valley the bleat of a lamb
in the vague hills behind her a man's voice
close by, the familiar breathing of her husband
in his sleep, her own heartbeat.
The stone fits exactly into her palm,
snuggles inside the furl of her fingers.
Her Galilee stone, she calls it
remembering the north country
evenings at olive gathering time
secrets opened with Mary.

Sometimes the weight of the stone
in her hand is a dead pain
a dumbness. Tonight she traces
its grained edges with her thumb
holds its smoothness against her cheek
brings it to her lips, feels its surface soften.
Only today she's seen there
the head of her unborn son:
the raised forehead, the indents
where the closed eyes nestle
the nose beginning, the small
slit mouth like a fish.

BEATITUDES

It was after the silence, some small crack opened in the rock.
His words: a scattering of feathers first, then
birds let loose below the high cliffs.

"Blessed are the poor in spirit," he said: "for they will have
the smells of the earth in their bones, will care
with a tallness not known to armies.

Blessed are those who mourn, their grief will open graves
carry home the broken bones, set loose
the horses of remembrance.

Blessed are the meek, flowers will open before them
the rigor mortis of the heart will melt
like ice before their eyes.

Blessed are those who are troubled with a restlessness
for justice, their tenacity will not buckle
before the tide's recurrent tumble.

Blessed are the merciful, they will suck chill from the marrow
of bent-over trees. They will be let linger
in the middle of their mercies.

Blessed are the pure in heart, their secrets will be whispered
as sap rising through tall trees, as shadows
holding tiny children in their sleep.

Blessed are the peacemakers, their remotest mountains
will gather together, touch fingertip to fingertip
till they are one single shone jewel.

Blessed are those who are persecuted in the cause of right,
thunderbolts that struck them will be broken
their darkness will be like shining."

Afterwards the silence gathered, closing the rock's small crack.
Blue crags turned the turquoise water white.
Strange birds flew in his dreams.

II

Not Written
on Stone

BURNING BUSH

Gershom had been restless with a broken sleep.
His teeth were coming.
Zipporah could no longer feed him from her breast.
I got up to comfort him, then
went back to lie beside her.
We lingered blissful in each other's delight.

It was then she felt the new tremor inside her.
"Quick, put your hand here." I felt nothing.
Later, langouring in semi-sleep
my hand still resting
along her belly
the movement came again.

I had spent the morning absent-minded among the cattle.
I was wrapped in tenderness: Zipporah's soft body
our Gershom with his huckleberry eyes, his gurgling
and that tiny kick against the inside of my wrist.

I was looking at the shape of Horeb, its slopes and shelves
the bushes with their hidden liturgies of bird-life
the grazing on the foothills
I watched without watching:

a pair of lambs suckling
their mother's concentrated indifference.
I was enraptured in the smallness of things.
Otherwise I might have missed it:

the beginnings of a shimmer
against the blue black of the mountain,
an almost flame.

There was no burning,
no crackle of fire feeding
on the brittle dried out branches
nor the fleshy fuzz of smoke.

It was at first
a yellow trigonometry of light;
brush strokes made by sheep or goats,
the smell of hoofprints; and then
the bush alive with transparent blue fire
like the delicate blaze of moon on frost.

It seemed like a stroke of sheep-wool on my chest;
a velvet purse inside my belly, a sorrow
too sweet to travel down my legs;
or the circle of a cormorant
diving in her wind-swept swoop
as she seeks her most immaculate of fishes.

And a storm held itself at ready,
hid in the vacuum between breezes
in the small shelter of my eyebrows;
its nowness
its unmeasured measurements
consuming me.
It was silent as milk.

A single lip-turn touched the fringes
of the air around me.
The flocks watched my wonderment
multiplying the silence.

Moses Moses Moses It came
like a mantra from the bush;
as if someone were making music
borrowing my name.

"I'm here" I said. "I'm here."
I didn't know what else to say.
It was then I took off my shoes
to hear what the ground was saying.

My feet naked on the earth
the felt calligraphy of grass.
I am your father's father.
(I had never known my father.)

I *am the wind-look, the sun-swept*
the language of land.
I became bewildered then.

I am   I am
That's all I can remember.
"I'm here" I said.

MIRROR OF LIGHT

Light-headed and hurried   my feet slipping
trying to catch up with myself   stopped on a ledge
breathless   my heart a drum   my legs shaking
a dank fog of nausea   in my belly   rising to my shoulders

Slowly   slowly   I told myself
lighter then   soon on the summit   facing south
the sun in my eyes   looking in a mirror of light
all I could see was dazzle

My breath in free-fall   I was wildflowers   a jonquil
the rock warm to my feet   the earth in my bones
the air   the scent of cedars

My speech fell to pieces   all stutter
sentences collided   words broke loose
turned to rubber   jumped like headless creatures
then gathered randomly   in heaps and clusters

Thought I heard God laughing
heard laughing   from my own belly

Quickly as they scattered the severed fragments of language
came into harmony   I said nothing then
there was no need for speech

God's eyes my eyes   within each other   seeing with one vision
together in our veins   in our measure of the mountain
moment followed moment   we knew everything

My legs apart   like trees growing   my hands
moving through air   as if flying
everything   spread out   particle by particle

My lips moist   my hair like feathers   the light
passing through my skin   God breathing
into me   out of me   all in one river

For three days   a mirror of light
God   one word only
a whisper
Moses

HOREB

The first time, I thought we were done for. When the men came
to my tent they were desperate. "Water. We have to have water."
There was less animosity in them than panic. I could handle that.
What bothered me more was the women. Their adulation.
And the trust on the children's faces, telling each other:
Moses is going to do something.

Worst of all were the animals. Their dumb looks could see
through me. It was mating season, yet even the rams were docile.
Cows stood mindlessly, their paps withered as dried figs.
A calf sucked my hand, its tongue rasping my knuckles
the roof of its mouth alabaster. A she donkey was bellowing
her urgent wails of parched music.

The eyes of the elders avoided me. One made the motion of
a spit as he shuffled past.

I prayed all that night. Towards dawn I slept a little, long enough
to dream. In the dream I am riding on my sister's shoulders with
my hands around her neck. She is running along the river bank
her long hair flying in my face. I can feel its wispy strands
between my lips. I am aged about four. She shows me the spot
where she hid me. The water moves swiftly.
The reeds are all shimmer.

Before daybreak I woke Aaron and the elders. We left silently
heading for Horeb.

I climbed alone, the rock cool under my feet. A piece of loose
slate rattled down the slope. In an hour I had reached a ledge
below the summit.

The sun rising, I could see the people breaking camp
family groups coming towards us like bunches of sage brush.
I could see myself as if from down there, a solitary figure
slanted against the morning.

I saw God then. That was the first time. It was only a glimpse. My body seemed all one limb. My arms, legs, chest, manhood were one piece; and the staff in my hand was alive.

I only touched the rock lightly when I struck it.

I heard the trickle of water above me. It sounded like women talking to each other; excited about something. Then I felt mist, like a slow smile along the length of my arm.

Below me I could see the faces looking up, and the animals breaking into a run.

A great applause of water was sweeping past me.

MIRIAM

The first time I met Aaron he talked of her. I'd imagined her then
lithe, with perfect rhythm of body and speech.
She was all of that, but she was beautiful as well.
Not so much her face but the way she held herself
her head thrown back, her long dark hair hanging
and the songs coming out of her.

They came from some place she couldn't find and wouldn't search for.
The words were ordinary. Any of us could have thought of them
but didn't. Her melodies were immediately familiar
and having heard them once we imagined
we had always known them.

She seemed to hear the songs that were hurting in us
then weave them back to us in ways we'd recognise.
She was forever humming to herself, and listening.
She picked up tunes from the wind blowing
through cedars, and tempo from
the flapping of a tent.

The words often came from conversation.
She turned speech rhythms into a refrain or anthem.
When she sang her whole body was in her voice,
and when she struck the tambourine
dark blood stirred in men
and the eyes of women lilted.

But this was as nothing
to what happened
when she danced.

I alone knew where the movements came from.
I watched her watch the quails come in the evening
the way they swerved, the way they let the manna fall
the shapes of the manna lying on the ground.
The Dance Of The Quails, the children loved that one best.

Sometimes she'd steal movements from the sandstorm
its swish and swirl, its long tailed disappearances.
The old ones loved *The Dance Of The Sandstorm*.
Nothing was too humble or profane
for her to learn some movement from:
a spear in flight, camels coupling,
the birth writhings of an antelope.

Miriam didn't meet God face to face as I did
but she prophesied in ways I couldn't
and she was close to God in ways not given to me.
She had a woman's way of seeing things I was blind to.
It was she who taught me the value of uncertainty
and to acknowledge doubt.

She turned against me once, in public, herself and Aaron.
It concerned my second marriage.
God did not hold it against them though he took my side
but it was Miriam's nature to hold it against herself.
She broke out in a rash so bad we feared leprosy
and although it disappeared, miraculously
she still quarantined herself.

We became even closer after that.
The fragility of friendship and the danger
of being swept from misunderstanding to estrangement
taught us to be patient in our listening,
to disagree with tenderness.

She and my first wife were always close.
Zipporah and I both noticed something was amiss with her:
a deadness in her voice, a sag along her shoulders.

The end came suddenly. There were no goodbyes.
Everything I said about her in the eulogy
I wish I'd said while she was still here.

Her burial was at Kadesh in the cool of evening.
When the line of sixteen men with tambourines
marched past the casket, it was a war going on
and when the line of women danced forward to the rhythm
it was peace restored. As darkness fell we sang her songs
and in the shadows cast by the new moon, her favourite pupil
the young woman with the dislocated hip, danced a sequence
of her best loved movements. Then she placed Miriam's slippers
face down on the grave-mound. Moonlit, their worn soles shone
like a dancer's shoulders, and like dancers bowing
seemed to kiss the earth to honour her.

Lastly as her oldest tambourine was placed beside them
a warrior came from the shadows
and plunged it with a spear.

That was the measure of our grief
and that was how we marked her resting place.
As we left we sang her song, *Deliverance*.

THE BALLAD OF BALAAM'S ASS

I like my boss Balaam, for better and worse
though I have to say he isn't bright.
His heart is well placed for most of the time
but his eyes aren't exactly alight.

He was wanted for blessings by many.
Balek the Moabite wanted a curse.
"Get rid of that Moses and all of his crew
and you'll surely be right well imbursed."

I tried to signal to Balaam
"don't touch it with a monkey hook."
But he was persuaded without too much fuss
and the order went into his book.

I saw the angel as soon as we moved
with his sword and the slant in his eye.
His purpose declared: to stop Balaam dead
as quick as my tail swats a fly.

'Twas my father taught me the following trick:
much better than turning about
go into a field, let on you're enticed
get a fistful of grass in your mouth.

My diversion didn't work, he just gave me a flake
had me up the boreen at a trot.
There was I, trying to dodge past the angel
with Balaam admiring the crop.

I could hear him hissing with temper
and he gave me a desperate clout
but the angel was waiting above in the gap.
This time there was no getting out.

I threw myself down, let on I was tired
but he beat me until I was cut.
My father's advice I then had to ignore:
"remember to keep your mouth shut."

I shouted a warning: "Balaam" says I.

31

That made him opened his eyes
saw the angel above with the sword in his hand
and was nearly struck dumb with surprise.

He never hit me again after that
and he's famous for oracles now.
He always asks for my opinion
and never a horse or a cow.

I give him the best of tuition.
Listen if you've any doubt.
Now he opens his eyes, and his ears
before letting his oracles out:

"I will not curse those that God will not curse
nor denounce those that God doesn't denounce."
"These people are rousing themselves like a lion.
They fight like an ox not a mouse."

I'll teach you to sing as good as yer man.
I'm starting an oracle class.
And if you enrol, either donkey or foal
your degree will be signed: *Balaam's Ass.*

FORTY YEARS ON

I was in my tent when it all started. I was thinking of Miriam:
the torn tambourine, the emptiness.
And that damn donkey braying me into a headache.

They were on about water. The lack of it.
Forty years, and still panicking about water.
I was weary of them.

I could see pomegranates shrivelled
beside the dried out river-bed.
Vines withered like old mens' veins.

I knew better than any how the flocks were suffering.
That morning I'd seen sheep
their bellies more bloated than at lambing time.

But these young men were concerned with comfort.
Their fathers, who survived on the spit of dried berries
brought their sons up soft.

Being lectured on leadership was not
what I expected. I threw them out.
That was a mistake.

I never said: "pomegranates my arse"
but I might as well have
such were the stories that went round.

Next morning outside my tent:
three hundred warriors in long lines of defiance
I could hear stones in their mouths.

Even the elders were sour and noncommittal.
They said antagonism could be done without.
They said Horeb was the only hope.

I was happy to go back there
but for the sake of stubbornness
I waited another two weeks.

I arranged it as before, setting out at dawn.
I asked Aaron if he'd climb with me.

We were slower this time around.

At last we found the rock-face
where the rust marks were.
We waited until everyone arrived.

Aaron says my harangue went on for half an hour
before I struck the rock one fierce defiant crack.
I don't remember that.

I remember my throat going dry,
the staff in my hand being a dead snake
and Aaron whispering: "strike it again, quick."

The staff began to wobble. I was dizzy.
The next thing a huge cheer went up.
They were singing a song I made with Miriam.

Water splashed across my shoulders.
Spray gathered in a blur around me.
I was grateful no one could see my face.

A WORN OUT DRUM

The men were singing and shouting; the women
dancing in snake-rings. I was a hero again.
I was the greatest thing since myself.

The young men bragged of how I'd put them down.
Mistaking arrogance for authority they honoured me
for the wrong reasons.

I wouldn't let Zipporah be a comfort.
My new wife did not swim deep.
Aaron was another country.

He walked around the camp oblivious
staring past himself. If someone asked
for his opinion he wouldn't give it.

Early one morning he said he was going to climb Mount Hor.
He asked me to come with him. Up there
he told me he wished to die alone.

It was Caleb who found him; sitting serenely
his back against a juniper tree.
We buried him in the exact spot.

I asked Joshua to speak.
He was generous in his praise
yet didn't gloss over flaws.

I was grateful for the young man's clarity
and lack of sentiment.
The mourning lasted forty days.

THE PROMISED LAND

During all of those years I struggled with despair.
It gathered like a dark vacuum in my belly
spreading up my chest and shoulders
and down the length of my arms.

My legs were ponderous as exhausted camels.
My failures came back to me: every wrong decision
every harsh judgement, the multitude of my doubtings.

My days were listless, my nights troubled
by unidentified dark creatures
gathered round me in mocking laughter.
The nightmares of my youth returned:

The Egyptian, his leering eyes
luminous under dark eyebrows
stalks my fellow tribesman.

He searches for a hiding place.
His breath comes in shallow gasps.
The Egyptian closes in, beats him without mercy.

My kinsman does not fight back.
He drops his hands, hoping for oblivion.
I try to shout encouragement.
The words come out in high-pitched whispers.
I can barely hear myself.

This dream kept recurring; night after night.
Then one night, as the Egyptian strikes my kinsman
my face begins to smart.
I can feel blood running from my lip.

Next thing I am circling the Egyptian.
He moves towards me, hits me twice
then twice again. He swings his arm back
to strike me to the ground.

Shimmying sideways I glide towards him
lock my arm around his neck
push it back, relentlessly
until I hear it snap.
I'm woken by the sound
of someone breaking firewood.

After this the dream changed:
The Egyptian is lying on the ground
his neck a broken fishing stick.

Night after night I try to bury him
but the wind blows the sand away.
His head keeps reappearing
the leer still fixed on his face.

Then I'm running, running.
The sand is slipping from under me
turning to salt, I cannot gain momentum.

I'm suffocating in my fear.
I know they'll find the body
discover it was I who killed him.

A boy appeared in the dream one night:
He is twelve years old, strong built.
He is standing on a stone stile.
He looks me in the eye.
He knows I did it.

Then no more dreams.
Just a deep black sleep
inside an endless darkness.
But my daytime depression began to lift.

Feelings would suddenly sweep over me
moments of unbearable sadness.
Seeing the frisking of lambs
or a couple courting
would bring a surge of tears.

One afternoon a child, about four years old
was playing near where I sat.
She came towards me

asked: "how old are you?"
I said: "you'll have to guess."
She said: "a hundred and forty years."

For the first time since I couldn't remember
I heard a chuckle coming from myself.
She clambered on my knee
stroked my beard
put her arms around my neck.
That's what did it.
I could talk to God again.

That night the dream came back:
This time I'm inside the Pharaoh's court
being tried for "crimes against humanity."
I have admitted guilt.

Where I am being held is underground.
The floor is covered in slime
the cell walls are plastered with animal dung.

My jailers lead me up the steps to hear the verdict.
The court is packed with hostile crowds.
The judge wears a huge black cloak.

He calls for silence. Then announces:
"Moses of the Israelites
you have been found guilty.
You are sentenced to life."

At that exact moment the Pharaoh
looks at me and winks.
It is Jethro my father-in-law
in disguise.

My jailers begin to cheer and clap me on the back.
I am lifted on their shoulders.
The hostile throng has become
people I have always known and loved.
I am carried out in triumph.

When I awoke I was different
and I have remained so since.

I'm not the man to lead this people
into the promised land.
God has helped me to this recognition
and affirms me in it.

I am too old now. And I am too at peace.
I know the people will not hear of this
but before God I have found myself unworthy.

I will prepare them for the crossing
remind them how far we've come
how fickle we all are, how we easily forget.

I will talk with God again
about his choice of leader.
I think it will be Caleb.

The happiest, saddest, most assuring thing for me
is knowing my life is ending,
that it has been everything it could be.
It was not better, or worse than others' lives.

The people will rejoice forever
in the memory of my triumphs.
I take comfort in the luxury of my failures.

Yesterday I saw an apple fall.
I brought it to my tent and held it.
It felt round and smooth.
I am content.

Soon I will be gathered up.
Tomorrow I will climb the hill
look across the river.

III

The Gift

This Morning

Inside: a soft dazzle,
imagined wine, Homer dark,
gliding toward the sun
my limbs like wax
warm to the flame.
Spring comes
early, window
to the blue summer.

And here, in my
very middle, heaven
spreads its small tremble
along each nerve, within
each vein, muscle:
mercury in the marrow.
Broken shells, shed skins
make this earth fertile.

Outside: tyre tracks
in the snow, the glitter
of galaxies, bear claws
on the monkey puzzle,
twigs turned to ghost
crocodiles
their snouts curved
their tongues tiny.

TREE

A tree grew
out of his belly last night
a tall tree with horny branches
and bark as tough as tusk
a trunk that would split iron
turn rodded steel to wire mesh

A rage roared
in his tree last night
from the moment of his navel
roared up the sinews
to its tall and leafy height
where birds gathered, air saluted air
and there was no hollow in the sturdy sky
roared down the dark shank
to where its roots rucked
as deep as they dared
as dug in to the darkness
as they did

And steel bands bent and broke
and rusted
as it spread its elbows
beside the waiting road

There was a grand arrogance
across its chest
and shoulders
at sunrise

WAGTAIL

Her narrow beak
carved finely
as a fish's fin

Her eyes
like tiny bubbles
duplicate the light

Her ankles
spindle-thin look best
in high-heeled shoes

Deftly she moves
fingertips the air
flirts her tail

Hesitates
then takes my
crust of bread

Then off
to bathe in
pools of rain

I dream
she calls me
on the phone

Her voice
is deep.

WINEGLASS

My eyes scan the tablescape
see hands move to salad bowls
take lettuce cucumber onion leek

A cluster of talk rises
and cutlery clatters on plates
like a shod horse trotting on cobbles

A pale breeze brushes
my lips   Your place
is empty

A wineglass stands
open-mouthed on the desk top
its stem still warm

I find you upstairs
your eyes wide rivers
your larynx

An ominous mound
between the taut
tendons of your throat

Behind you
the wall is bruised
where you banged your head

"I'll tear that man
to pieces" you say
your teeth clenched

Your fists pound
the drums below my collarbones
till your hands ebb open

Downstairs   I take the glass
rinse away
the smudge of blood.

DREAMWEAVER

Her Celtic hair
wild wisps of heather
on a Galway hill.

"Have you ever noticed how your nails
pick out the pigment of your skin?" she said
showing me: hers first
how eggshell white picks out translucencies

then mine, highlighting the tangle of blue briars
from my knuckles to my wrist
the deep tan between my thumb and fingers
shadowlands, a string quartet.

I shall step out of my singular shoes
rest inside that curve, her clavicle
bottleneck of desire
the snow's seventh white.

She, dreamweaver
beyond belief, hymenopterous
in the virile light.

FAMINE

During the winter is the worst time.
You can see my footprints across the field
you can tell I'm strange.
Then I have to hide again, turn sallow
blend with the contours of the mist
turn blue like the drizzled grass.

Like a fieldmouse hunched in rushes
I watch the well, where they come
with pairs of buckets.
And with hair hung down like briars
I hide in the long ditches
enduring hunger, cold, and scratches.

In summertime I feed on mushrooms
blackberries, sometimes the smallest of rabbits
and eels I find wriggling in the silt
as it oozes from the peat.

Where you have not searched
I hear the voice of ploughman and of heifers.
I hide the thin jut of my jaw
between the sharp edged stones on ditches.

The furze is my field
yellow as the white of my eyes.
And when the summer comes
I hide under the skin of earth

among grass roots
below the hawthorne hedge
beside the house of yellow hammers
half way between the road and river.

BEYOND

The first thing I knew
was seeing the blood
thinning itself in the water
turning the river pink.

The next thing I saw
was a shoal of limbs
gliding below the surface
like a tangle of branches

and then
the severed heads
half buoyant, sinking and rising
as if bouncing on the river-bed.

One turned face up, as it sped
past the spot where I stood;
its cheeks still ruddy,
its black beard saluting me.

Across the open field
a young woman is running.
Her face is colourless
with fear.

I show her a hiding place
beyond the white-washed wall.
I stand, holding my breasts in my palms.
They are hard as stones.

To Grief's End

Far out
      she rode
            proudly

Gliding
      over seaweed
            rock

Her hair
      flamboyant
            laughing

Now
      her death rattle
            rasping through shingle.

50TH BIRTHDAY

Nagasaki
 The clatter of clouds
  The sea rolling back
   Inch by fuzzy inch
    Swallowing time
     Tormenting the shadows

INTERRUPTION

I was combing your hair before the rolling mirrors
    You were wrapping my almond cheeks in your hands
        Our eyes were a gathering of barnacles

We were flying the tangle of miles
    Above the blue eager hills
        Across a calendar of rivers

            When the telephone rang

JACK RABBIT

I could have it easy if I knuckled down
he said; it was up to myself.
I knuckled down all right
but not the way he meant.
That went on for five years.
In the end he moved out.

Afterwards, whenever we'd meet, say at a funeral
we were civil enough. We'd shake hands
him looking past my shoulder
searching some outer hemisphere
and innocent as a satellite dish
picking up my frequencies with his ear.

When I asked him: "How's Kitty?" he said:
"Didn't you bury her last year." That cheered him up.
He died himself awhile back
and wherever he is now I'll bet
he's talking about me.
Not that I'd ever talk about him.

He hasn't appeared to me yet, as far as I know.
But last night in Edmonton
at thirty two below, a jack-rabbit
bounded like a huge white shadow
across my headlights
and disappeared in the snow.

FOR THE LOVE OF BUDS

I love them more than leaves waving across high transepts,
that cool the sweat at the back of the neck, and at dusk
become lace curtains; (I most love leaves
in their open-handed hovering, their rustling farewell,
their mournful winter-gone).

I love buds more than twigs, with their fine skin
and fingers pointing heavenward;
or branches, thick-wristed and elbowed
all clenched fist and biceps; or barrel-chested trunks
with skin of scale and scallop shell.

I love them more than roots facing the darkness bravely,
(though roots can hear and grip, and are ancient as November.)
Buds are young. Their eyes still blind they seek the light for anchor.
They scent their way, tuck out their green-tipped tongues
for tastes of rainfall.

I love the full and green of summer hedge.
I like the tall tree shelter.
I like a long and leafy ledge.
I love buds more, and better.

COMMUNION ROUND

for Minnie Herlihy

You're better than you were
when you woke up; you say
your short straight legs protruding from your chair.

I must have been working nights.
I must have been taking
those penalties England missed.

Last week we saw you celebrate
your birthday, your 78th.
This week you're watching the World Cup.

Oh I always loved my sport.
A runner when I was at school.
Aye, and I was fast.

You sit there now, your joints
arthritis-locked. Taking penalties!
As I begin the prayers a chuckle comes.

This turns to tenderness
when I see -dare I mention it- your wig.
That's when the poem begins.

Outside: I see bunches of asparagus
fully grown and six feet tall
hear the traffic pass; through tears

I marvel how you disregard the clock:
the yellow, blue, and turquoise
flowers on your frock.

READING RUMI IN THE RED BEAR

The study of this book will be painful for those
who feel separate from God

The landlord, his ponytail curving
towards the till pulls someone's pint
then comes to take my order.
He rings it through to Susan.

Who says words with my mouth?
Who looks out with my eyes?

An elder in the alcove, her hair
the yellow side of white, drinks pints and smokes.
She talks about the morning: what she did
what the other woman said.

Be empty of worrying
think of who created thought

Through the window by the traffic lights
a man laughs, amused at what he's seeing
his tooth-gap shares the joke.
Rumi says: *feel the delight*

of walking in the noisy streets,
and being the noise

In the oak-panelled dining room
heart-shaped stools with matching tables.
On the wall a framed stallion
held forever by a stable lass.

Flow down and down, in always
widening rings of being

A surge of silver blurs my eyes.
Susan brings the scampi and chips.

SUFFERINGS

I talked sedately
about love: how the grass
grows in the freedom
of God's forever

how each name is
sung, sweet
as the blackbird you heard
before the early worm

and how every hurted thing
is made into
the image of a king.

Afterwards, he caught me like the sweep of a scythe; said
I never mentioned the other side, never a word
about the sufferings of Christ. His rr's rolled
in a great skirl, leaving shivers
resonant in the air.

                       I saw what he meant
as my sermon lay dying. There
cloudless as lace, despair bunched
on his daughters' shoulders
the sufferings of Christ
on his wife's face.

SCARTHINGWELL PARK

Still recovering from last week's fall
Molly's forehead is an autumn coloured bruise.

Would you like communion? *Yes Please.*
What day is it?

> *-hallowed be thy name, thy kingdom come*
> *-give us this day our daily bread*

I forget what age I am.
I was born in 1882, I think
how old would that be?
Is this Oxfordshire?

My son is in the navy.
That's him over there
and that's my grandson's wedding.
Have you met my family?

What day is it?

Outside, on the lake
three Canada geese diverge
leaving separate silver wakes.
In the narrow lane the last leaves fall.

It's Friday.

LAST WORDS OF ANDREW T.

Who gave that hedge-clipper to the grasshopper?
The heifers are coming for the hayfield
stand in the gap with my hat on.

Would I know her? I would, boiled in porridge.
Two and two four and two eight and four ten
another two loads and you'll have it all in.

Four years old and do you know what she said:
"Daddy will you do me a favour?"
I've a daughter married, and another in a job.
And a son above in Sligo.

Who have I?
Is that you Micky boy, when did you come?
Over in England. Yerra, no good.

They have the place surrounded. Shsss
quick, quick gimme the gun.

Look, that britchin is dragging, tighten the girth.
You'll find the whittletree below in *Conaic Na Muc.*
Good man. Pull hard on the reins now
face her straight for the ditch.

Give out the rosary now-so; a decade a man.
Stop. Start that again.
Hail Mary full of grace, pray for us now and at the hour of
half past ten. That clock is five minutes fast.
Holy Mary Mother of Sep-
timber and not a sod of turf in the house.
Pray for us. Pray for us. Pray for us.

The Grangerbreakers are at it again.

I'll walk beside you through the world tonight.
Will we have the honeymoon above in Cahercon?
We'll be late for the funeral if you don't hurry on.
I think I'll stop where I am.

TOM THE TRAVELLER
For Frances

She doesn't come running to the door with hugs.
It's not her style. She watches robin-like
and when I've passed the test
she asks me out to play.

She shows me her new garden first.
We chase each other, each in turn and then
she takes me by the hand
to see her horse.

She climbs into the saddle, takes the reins
tells me sit up behind. We gallop off to everywhere,
down past Cappoquin, back along Blackwater valley
her cut-down branch the fastest horse since Pegasus.

Later, you and I drink tea. You say
"she's got her brother on a piece of string
just like I had you;" recalling how
you used to trump my every trick
by threatening: "I'll tell."

And you tell me how you bring them to his grave sometimes
and wonder: what would he have thought of them?
and last time you wondered:
what would they have thought of him?

He liked to read the paper first
uninterrupted
the headlines, then the deaths.
But you would climb inside his elbow
to check out Tom the Traveller.
It was the one cartoon he'd countenance.
He'd ask you to interpret it
then laugh out loud; marvel at your wit.

Between us on the table
a teapot
bowl of sugar
jug of milk

the distance paper thin.

BLESSING

I bless you in the name of the morning
the first thing of it, whispering
through the folds of my ear-imprinted pillow.
In the name of the mirror, toothbrush
and the slow shower that clarifies
vowels and consonants of my waking.

I bless you in the name of the breakfast
the wake up of it, orange juice and
Quaker Oats, sometimes Cornflakes
milk, white and breathless
becoming supple flesh of sally-rod
bone of unbreakable dolomite.

I bless you in the name of toast, buttered
and spread flat, not to mention marmalade
its orange ribs rolled into this glass jar.
And in the name of an egg, boiled
in a white fountain-head of bubbles
the shell cracked open, and salted.

I bless you in the name of the chair, upright
my feet soft-shod on the floor-shine.
In the name of Gerry, who lives downstairs
and makes no more noise than a mouse
and in the name of the mouse
for whose absence I am grateful.

I bless you in the name of the marigold sun
remembering me to the meadows, where cows
who neither know nor number, graze
in a mist that is minding its own business
as it rises over the river
disappearing until nightfall.

I bless you in the name of the air
rising over my childhood
when I stood to my waist in the water
splashed in a sacrament of swimming.
Where I ran round the field with my sister
in her summer of first communion.

I bless you in the name of that summer
for girls who came down from the city
and our games played in white clover.
Once and for all and over and over
for moments of eternity
here and now, and forever. Amen.

In Memoriam

Let's say the year is twenty-one-sixteen.
The headstone says I died in twenty-thirty-six.
Though I've been dead these eighty years
I'm pleased to see I lived to ninety one.

The graveyard perched
above an S of sea where boats can rest
along a lonely curve of shore
where tourists no longer come.

Beneath my name: the dates of birth and death,
some long-forgotten lines I haven't written yet.
Beside my grave a grass-grown gravel path
unused except by fishermen at night.

I see a woman, pushing back the grass.
She's twenty-five or so.
Researching for her PhD, her subject:
Forgotten Irish Poets.

She found some poems of mine on micro-disk
buried in the archives of a library
in Edmonton Alberta, where
I was almost famous once.

She stands among small raindrops
as I once stood
in the graveyard at Drumcliff.
She weeps as I wept over Yeats.

A strand of hair clings to her face.
A briar sways in unnoticed wind.
Far below the waves say hush.
Close by a blackbird sings.

THE GIFT

And love, she said, was not
waiting for what had been expected
but more like listening to the river
that ran beneath your skin

was not the silver birch
spine stiff with anticipation
but more like the shiver of its leaves
upturned in the mid-morning wind.

And love, she said, was not
the breaking of some stone ghost
but more like the sound of water ebbing.
It came, she said, like a slow tide.

It crept across the shadows of trees
through the open skylight
into the bedroom of the boy
while his memory lay sleeping.

It came, she said
touching the space between his eyebrows,
fixing in his dark dreams
the broken axle to the wheel.

AFTER THE WEDDING

I leave the revellers at midnight.
Southbound on the M6 the phone rings
and before answering it, I know.

At 9.30pm tonight my mother died.

The car cruises, the curve of the wipers
responding to sporadic showers.
My engines have shut down.

Dull at the edges, raw in the centre
I can feel my toes tingle.
Yesterday she sat out in the sun.

I wait an hour, then call you.
I hear the texture of your voice
as you retell each moment slowly.

This morning she said to you "I'm dying"
and you asked "are you afraid?"
She told you she was not.

After the priest had come and blessed her
with the final rites, the day went quietly.
She slept a little now and then.

In the evening she told Ita she was going.
"Maybe I'll wait until the morning."
In the event she didn't.

At 95 years, and conscious to the last
her breathing stopped. I ask about
distress. You say there was none.

Arriving home at 3.00am, there are
nine messages on my Ansaphone.
I don't need to answer them.

I check the Internet for flights, then walk outside.
In a while I hear the first birds sing.
Memories begin.